*Lush foliage in
the palm oasis at
Andreas Canyon,
near Palm Springs,
California.*

DESERT PALM OASIS

Text and Photographs by
James W. Cornett

Curator of Natural Science
Palm Springs Desert Museum

Palm Springs Desert Museum
101 Museum Drive
Palm Springs, California 92263

This publication and the research it represents were made possible by a grant
from the Richard King Mellon Foundation of Pittsburg, Pennsylvania.
The author would like to thank the Agua Caliente Band of Cahuilla Indians
and The Nature Conservancy for their assistance on this project.

Produced for the Palm Springs Desert Museum by
Companion Press
Santa Barbara, California
Jane Freeburg, Publisher/Editor

*Designed by Lucy Brown
Copyedited by Cheryl Jeffrey
Printed and bound in Korea
through Bolton Associates, San Rafael, California*

ISBN 0-944197-10-8

CONTENTS

*An old and dying
desert fan palm at
Cantu Palms, Baja
California Norte.*

5

CHAPTER ONE:

The Desert Fan Palm Discovered

"Spreading up from Northern Mexico, a number of groups of the fan palm, Washingtonia filifera, *are found in the canyons and oases of the Colorado Desert. They are known to but few, and those are mainly prospectors and such stray characters, whose business or hobby makes them wanderers in that harsh region."*

— J. Smeaton Chase, 1919

The Colorado and Mojave Deserts of California are the driest environments in North America. Localities within Joshua Tree National Monument, for example, receive less than four inches of rainfall annually. Park rangers at the visitor center in Death Valley National Monument record less than two inches of precipitation in most years. The impact of this aridity is made more profound by intensely hot summers. Borrego Springs, in the center of California's Anza-Borrego Desert State Park, endures an average daily maximum temperature in July of 110° F but takes a back seat to Death Valley, where July afternoons average a whopping 116° F.

With such intense heat and so little moisture, the potential evaporation is more than ten times the actual precipitation — leaving little water for plants, animals or humans. Without water, life cannot exist. Thus it is small wonder that the first impression of the desert is one of emptiness. Thousands of square miles of rock, sand, and dwarf shrubs dominate the terrain. To the lost and thirsty prospector of bygone days, the arid landscape must have seemed endless.

This region should be the last place where one would expect to find dense groves of water-loving palm trees. Yet such groves do exist complete with shade, relatively cool temperatures and life-giving water. At the heart of these oases is the most massive palm in North America, the desert fan palm *Washingtonia filifera;* a palm whose numbers in the wild approach 25,000 and whose range extends from the Baja Peninsula to Death Valley National Monument.

The Discovery

Indians clearly knew of the existence of palm trees on the desert for hundreds, if not thousands, of years. Ancient Indian villages and campsites have been located at many oases, and the palm tree is a common element in the oral traditions of the Cahuilla Indian peoples of southeastern California.

However, in 1789 wild desert palms were unknown to European explorers. Spanish soldier Pedro Fages first wrote about them and is thus credited with their "discovery". Fages' diary describes the event:

"We set out . . . in the morning following the same dry stream, winding to the westward. After we had gone four leagues, we found a small spring of good water, near which there were three or four very tall palm trees . . . "

Fages had departed from "La Conception" (near present-day Yuma) in early

*Opposite:
Palm Canyon, near Palm Springs, California, is the largest desert fan palm oasis with 2,511 adult trees in 1986.*

April of 1782, headed for the San Gabriel mission near what we now call Los Angeles. However, upon learning of Indian disturbances to the south, he changed his plans and headed toward San Diego so that he and his men might encounter and quell any hostile natives. Historian E. I. Edwards has shown that Fages struck a route through the Carrizo Corridor in modern-day Anza-Borrego Desert State Park. The palms Fages encountered surrounded a waterhole in that corridor; a spring that would later be named Palm Spring (not to be confused with the famed desert resort of Palm Springs in Riverside County, California.)

Fages' account was the first mention of palm trees in the West, and it would certainly not be the last. But sixty-five years passed before desert palms reappeared in the literature. This time it was an Anglo-American, Lt. Col. William H. Emory , who wrote in 1848 of the palms:

"A few miles from the springs called Ojo Grande, at the head of the creek, several scattered objects were seen projected against the cliffs . . . They were cabbage trees and marked the locale of a spring and a small patch of grass."

Lt. Col. Emory was a topographic engineer accompanying General Stephen Kearny's Army of the West as it headed to the Pacific Coast. For weeks the troops had been struggling across the deserts of Arizona and California where water was always in short supply. The men quickly learned that green foliage on the desert could indicate a spring. One can easily imagine their exhilaration when they spotted a verdant palm oasis situated against a pale, barren hillside on the morning of November 28, 1846. At the oasis they found not only palms but a pool of water and a small meadow in which their horses could feed. In fact, Kearney's men had happened upon the same oasis at which Pedro Fages had found refuge sixty-five years before.

An interesting facet concerning the discovery of the Desert Fan Palm is the

Five Palms in Borrego Badlands, Anza-Borrego Desert State Park, is one of the few oases where palm numbers have declined in the last four decades.

curious history of their changing numbers at Palm Spring itself. Fages mentioned that he found "three of four very tall palm trees" at the spring in 1782. Col. George Cooke, who stopped at the spring on January 17, 1847, wrote in his journal that they found "twenty or thirty palm trees" at the spring. It would seem that either Fages and Cooke were talking about two different palms oases (an explanation refuted by Edwards in 1961) or the number of palms at Palm Spring has increased almost tenfold in sixty-five years. Was such an increase possible? Perhaps, but by 1850 every palm at Palm Spring had been cut down by prospectors, settlers, and employees of the Butterfield Overland stageline which had built a waystation at the spring in that year.

Visitors to the oasis today will find palms again at the waterhole. The three trees there are the result of plantings by Anza-Borrego Desert State Park rangers, who in the early 1960s wished to return

Above: Dos Palmas Spring, east of the Salton Sea, is located below sea level.

Left: Fossil of a fan palm leaf, about 8 million years old, found in southern California. Palms as a group have existed in western North America for at least 40 million years. However, no fossils of the desert fan palm, Washingtonia filifera, *have ever been found.*

Palm Bowl, in Anza-Borrego Desert State Park, is reached by a 2-kilometer hike. The oasis is unusual in that the number of adult palms (82) has remained about the same for the past thirty-five years.

palms to the spring and thereby restore the natural vegetation. Unfortunately, the well-intentioned rangers erringly planted seeds of Mexican Fan Palms, *Washingtonia robusta*, a non-native species restricted to the central Baja Peninsula. Perhaps someday the rightful Desert Fan Palm, *Washingtonia filifera*, will reign over the oasis again.

Naming the New Palm

Some of Kearny's soldiers, familiar with the Cabbage Palmettos (*Sabal palmetto*), of the Carolinas and Florida, saw the fan-shaped leaves of the palms at Palm Spring and called the new palms "cabbage trees." Kearny's men had found not cabbage trees, but a plant whose affinities had not yet been determined nor a scientific name assigned. Thirty more years would pass before this would occur.

In 1869, a naturalist named R. Roezl acquired seeds of the desert fan palm while on an expedition in the western United States. There being no customs officials or agricultural inspectors at that time, Roezl was able to return to Europe with the seeds in his possession. He sold the seeds to Lucian Linden, a plant dealer from Ghent, Belgium. Unfortunately, Roezl did not relate precisely where the seeds came from (the type "locality"). Their place of origin is obscure and the subject of some debate.

Linden planted a few seeds and listed the remaining ones for sale in his seed catalog. In his publication he used the name *Pritchardia filifera*, and thus became the first person to affix a scientific name to the species. But Linden's designation was conservative; he elected to place the new palm in the well-known genus *Pritchardia* which also had fan-shaped leaves. (By modern standards his choice was also rather arbitrary, since leaf form often changes with the age of the plant and with the conditions under which the plant grows. Leaf form also does not show the intricate variability so typical of flowers, the structure now used to classify plant species.) Linden's classification would not last under the scrutiny of German botanist Herman Von Wendland.

Wendland visited Lucian Linden sometime in the late 1870s. After examining Linden's young palms he wrote, in a research paper published in 1879, that the palms should not have been placed in the genus *Pritchardia*. Rather, they represented not only a new species but an entire new genus of palm as well. Wendland named the genus *Washingtonia*, in honor of America's first President. As was the custom in erecting a new genus, he kept the second part of the binomial name, *filifera*, used by Linden; a word taken from Latin which described the thread-like fibers that curled about the leaf edges and tips of Linden's specimens. The proper form used today thus bears the name of both men "*Washingtonia filifera* (Linden) Wendland." Linden is given credit for first applying a scientific name to the species but Wendland is considered to have correctly classified it and his new genus has become accepted by botanists the world over.

Two curious footnotes end the story of the discovery and naming of the Desert Fan Palm. Although Wendland had the priviledge of naming the palm, he never saw one in its natural habitat; nor did he ever see a photograph or sketch of one in the wild. Further, the only specimens he had on which to base his new genus were several immature palms, without flowers or fruit. Most modern botanists would consider this an insufficient morphological basis on which to erect a new genus. Apparently, Wendland couldn't wait the twelve to fifteen years it required for the specimens to reach maturity!

Above: Grapevine Canyon, in Death Valley National Monument, is the most northerly location of desert fan palms.

Right: Desert fan palms are widely distributed, with oases found in Southern California, Baja California Nortè, Southern Nevada, and Western Arizona.

Death Valley
National Monument

UTAH

Las Vegas

NEVADA

Needles

Twentynine Palms

Los Angeles

Palm Springs

COLORADO RIVER

Borrego Springs

Salton Sea

RIVER

San Diego

CALIFORNIA

BAJA   CALIFORNIA

Yuma

GILA

ARIZONA

SONORA

Ensenada

PACIFIC OCEAN

San Felipe

Gulf of California

✱   DESERT FAN PALM OASIS

⌒   COLORADO DESERT BOUNDARY

Lone Palm is located in Joshua Tree National Monument – at 3950 feet, the highest elevation where desert fan palms occur naturally. This 5-foot tree is over 50 years old, but has never reached maturity due to the cold weather at this elevation. The tree probably grew from a coyote-dropped seed brought from Fortynine Palms further down the canyon.

Below: The American Robin may be an important disperser of palm seeds.

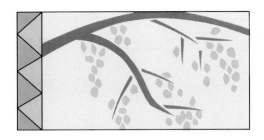

Chapter Two:

Knowing The Palm

"There is a reserved majesty and beauty in the form of the desert palm which has aroused great admiration . . . "

— Edmund C. Jaeger, 1969

The desert fan palm is one of the tallest native plants of the Sonoran Desert and the largest palm in North America. Mature individuals are known to reach twenty-five meters in height and attain a trunk diameter approaching one meter. The desert fan palm is also the only palm in the world whose dead leaves remain affixed to the trunk throughout its life.

Considered a fast-growing species, a typical desert fan palm adds about thirty centimeters of trunk per year. This rate is maintained for about the first twenty years. After that the growth rate decreases steadily. Trees over fifteen meters in height grow very slowly, probably not more than two to four centimeters per year. At sites where water supplies are limited, such as at Pygmy Grove in Anza-Borrego Desert State Park, or where climate conditions are relatively cold as at Grapevine Springs in Death Valley

National Monument, even young palms may add just five or six centimeters each year.

The most rapid growth rate I have recorded was in Thousand Palms Oasis near Palm Springs, California. A tree there developed a three-meter trunk in six years. It grew in the shade of numerous other palms and had germinated in a warm spring. These two factors were undoubtedly the causes of its rapid growth. Palms in shaded conditions grow faster and have narrower trunks than those in full sun and the warm water undoubtedly helped maintain steady growth through the cold winter months.

The most distinctive characteristic of the desert fan palm is the skirt of dead leaves or "petticoat" which can completely obscure the trunk. Unlike every other palm species in the world, the leaf stems or "petioles" of the desert fan palm typically adhere to the trunk throughout its life. Such a "virgin" palm appears larger since the dead hanging leaves can add another two meters to the tree's diameter.

The trunk is revealed when the leaf skirt or "petticoat" has been burned away or, in rare instances, if unusually high winds have blown the skirt off or floods have torn it away. In the latter two cases the gray-brown palm bark, with its cross-hatched surface of tiny vertical and horizontal crevices, may be exposed. These scars show where the leaf bases were once attached. The term palm bark is technically inaccurate because the outer layer of a palm is not really bark as is found on the exterior of conifers and dicot trees such as pinyon pines, cottonwoods and sycamores. True bark is created by a thin cylindrical outer cambium cell layer, near the exterior of these trees. (The inner cambium produces wood cells inwardly, causing the trunk to increase in diameter as the tree grows.) The outer cambium ring produces bark cells that protect the delicate tissues beneath. The cracked and gnarled

Opposite: Monsen Canyon, in Joshua Tree National Monument, is one of the least-visited palm oases. At close to 3,900 feet in elevation, the palms in the upper portion of the canyon are among the highest palms.

15

surface of a conifer or dicot tree is the old cambium-produced cork cells that are sloughed off as the trunk expands. Palms have no cambium growth rings and so possess no true bark, nor do they increase their diameter after the leaves and crown have attained their full size.

In conifer and dicot trees, tiny vertical tubes of vascular tissue lie alongside the cambium layer. The vascular tissue is responsible for transporting water and nutrients up and down the trunk. As mentioned above, palms and other monocots lack this circular cambium layer but of course still require vascular tissue. In palms this tissue is located in hundreds of bundles that are dispersed throughout the trunk, not just near the periphery. This feature of palms is important to remember since it is a primary reason why palms are so adept at surviving fire. It also means that palms, as well as other perennial monocots, do not have annual growth rings from which their age can be determined.

The desert fan palm increases the height of its trunk by producing new leaves at its growing tip, or apical meris-

tem. New leaves emerge vertically from the meristem and are then pushed aside as more leaves emerge. The trunk is made taller by this process and the "palm bark" is what can be seen if the petioles break off or are trimmed away from the trunk. The apical meristem can be considered the most important part of the desert fan palm. The trunk, leaves, and roots can sustain appreciable amounts of damage but if the lone growing tip is injured, the palm dies. Although date palms (*Phoenix* spp.) can grow sprouts from their root crowns, the desert fan palm has no such ability.

The increase in trunk diameter of young palms results from the widening of the trunk just below the apical meristem. The growth form is initially something akin to an inverted cone, except the roots grow from the bottom which stabilizes the expanding cone and gives the base a columnar appearance. One can usually see the juncture of the roots and the trunk on wild desert fan palms.

Many people assume that all perennial desert palms have long taproots that reach moisture deep underground, but desert fan palms have no taproot. On the contrary,

Castle Creek Palms, near Wickenburg, Arizona, is the eastern-most desert fan palm location.

like most monocots, palms have fibrous systems. In the case of palms, these are composed of thousands of pencil-width rootlets that are rarely more than five meters in length. (The longest desert fan palm root I have ever measured was ten meters and grew from one of the trees at Sheep Hole Palms, Riverside County, California. The water table had been dropping at this site for several years and the palm had extended its roots into an adjacent wash in search of moisture.) The root mass is so dense that the roots of other competing plant species seldom if ever can penetrate the soil space occupied by the palm. These root masses are conspicuous when nursery-grown desert fan palms are dug up prior to being transplanted.

Fronds and Flowers

Although all of the world's 2,800 or so palm species belong in the plant family known as Arecaceae, *Washingtonia filifera* is also a member of a subgroup termed the Coryphoid palms; a division that includes the genera *Brahea, Livistonia, Pritchardia,*

and *Sabal.* A key feature of the subgroup is the fan-shaped or palmate leaf, best displayed in *Washingtonia.* Desert fan palm leaves or "blades" can be nearly two meters long, with a comparable width, and resemble a huge fan with forty to sixty accordian-like folds. Typically, each leaf remains functional for about one year, turns brown, then becomes part of the petticoat.

The flattened petiole, or leaf stalk, can be up to two meters long and, in palms under ten meters in height, is armed with rows of wicked spines on the two edges. These spines are dangerously sharp and can easily rip apart human skin as can be attested by a friend who had been hiking with me in Andreas Canyon near Palm Springs. He slipped on a rock at the edge of a stream and made the mistake of grabbing a palm petiole to stop his fall. The resultant gash across his palm required fourteen stitches to close. It has been reported that a toxic compound covers the petiole spine and can result in intense inflammation to the wound and surrounding tissue. However, no such

Above, left: Fountain grass, tamarisk and fan palms compete for water and space at Dead Indian Canyon.

Right: Sharp spines on the petiole of a fan palm can be dangerous. They probably evolved as protection against large herbivores during the Pleistocene.

complications occurred in the instance described above nor in my own minor accidents involving desert fan palms.

I confess that I have never actually counted all the blossoms on a desert fan palm. However, counts of flower stalks, or spadices, on several hundred palms (and counts of flowers on a few large spadices) indicate that healthy palms produce up to fourteen spadices, each with up to 400,000 flowers. Thus an extremely robust palm could have up to six million flowers — clearly heaven for a nectar-seeking insect.

However, most palms do not produce fourteen spadices. Young palms do not produce any spadices until they have reached a height of three to four meters. *Washingtonias* growing in crowded groves or with poor moisture resources will not produce any spadices at all.

The first year a palm reaches maturity it produces less than five fruit stalks, increasing the number to fourteen stalks at eight or nine meters in height. Tall, old trees may manage only a single spadix.

Counts of several hundred trees indicate that the average number of spadices per mature individual is seven. However, recently-burned palms produce an average of eleven and ornamental desert fan palms produce thirteen. These latter two instances of increased spadix production seem to be the result of an abundant and continuous supply of water. A stroll through an oasis after a fire usually reveals that there is more moisture at the surface; a result of temporary elimination of the plants that normally intercept the water before it reaches ground level. Ornamental palms, of course, receive regular watering. Curiously, although palms only occur at sites of permanent water availability, years of below-average precipitation result in a decrease in spadix production. This suggests that the palms, and perhaps other oasis plants as well, are tapping the maximum amount of moisture available and are moderately stressed during unusually dry years.

Top: Desert fan palm flowers. Up to five million may be produced by a single palm.

Center: The Carpenter Bee feeds on palm flowers, often damaging them. The female bees often lay their eggs in desert fan palm trunks, within exit holes formed by palm boring beetles.

Bottom: Ripe palm fruit appears in fall.

Spadices reach four meters in length, usually branch at least once, and appear as early as January (in Surprise Canyon, Anza-Borrego Desert State Park) though typically they are first noticed in late May. They emerge near the center of the crown immediately above a petiole. Flower clusters first split the spadix sheaths in early June and by late June blooming is well underway. Blooming continues into July in Kofa Palm Canyon, Arizona.

The flowers have both male (three stamens) and female (one pistil) parts. Flowers are never more than ten millimeters in length. Under a dissecting microscope, the three whitish petals can be seen to be bent backwards upon themselves in a deflexed position. Although a very healthy palm may produce over five million flowers, the majority of the blossoms are destroyed by bees, specifically carpenter bees (*Xylocopa*), that bite the flowers off in their quest for nectar. The bounty of insects that are attracted to the flower clusters would suggest that the desert fan palm is insect, rather than wind, pollinated. Individual palms are also known to pollinate themselves.

The number of flowers that survive and develop into mature fruits never approaches the number of flowers produced. The rough treatment of carpenter bees, the heavy winds that strip blossoms from the spadices, and the uncertainty of pollination results in at least 90% of the flowers failing to develop into fruit. My counts suggest that even the healthiest tree does not produce more than 350,000 seeds, or about 27,000 seeds per spadix.

Desert fan palm fruits are straw colored during their early development, and can be observed hanging in dense

Violent summer thunderstorms create rushing torrents, such as this one in Palm Canyon near Palm Springs.

Inset: Palm trunks may be damaged by flood-propelled boulders, as was this tree within the Boyd Deep Canyon Desert Research Center.

clusters from the crown. By midsummer the fruits have turned green and by October the fruits have ripened and turned black. The fruit covering, the exocarp, is jet black. Just-ripened fruits are covered with a thin syrup-like substance that is sticky to the touch and attracts many insects. At this time, the fruits easily affix to hands or clothing.

Most of the fruits are knocked off the stalks by wind or birds and fall to the ground. Only under unusual circumstances, such as a fallen palm or a palm growing to the top of a canyon wall, do the clusters hang sufficiently close to ground level that they can be reached by coyotes or foxes. If the fruits fall on moist soil—particularly moist, sunlit soil—they may germinate in less than five days. Germination time is slowed, or prevented altogether, if the exocarp has not been removed or at least been damaged.

The early growth of a desert fan palm is typical of a monocot — a single leaf or cotyledon emerges from the seed, followed quickly by a second leaf. These leaves may enlarge tremendously, sometimes attaining widths in excess of two inches and lengths of up to twelve inches under shaded conditions. In sunny conditions it appears that the first distinctive fan-shaped leaves develop sometime within the first year.

Desert fan palms are the most cold-resistant palms in the world. This tree in Chino Canyon, near Palm Springs, wears a winter dusting of snow.

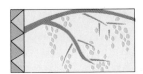

*Located in the
remote Kofa
Mountains of
northwestern
Arizona, the palms
of Fishtail Canyon
are different than
palm populations
elsewhere. Kofa
Mountain palms
may represent the
only relict
populations of
Washingtonia
filifera.*

CHAPTER THREE:

Indians and the Fan Palm

From 1982 through 1988 I visited 135 of the 151 desert fan palm oases in California, Baja California Norte, southern Nevada and Arizona. Although my research was directed toward discovering recent factors that affect the size of palm groves, one of my most consistent findings — at approximately 70% of the oases — was the material remains of Indians associated with the palm oases.

Potsherds and lithic materials were the most frequently encountered objects. They were found at the mouths of canyon oases or at elevated terraces or ridges; rarely was anything found in canyon bottoms. This is not surprising in light of the fact that most palm groves are subject to flash floods and objects in canyon bottoms are swept away along with many of the palms during severe cloudbursts.

Bedrock mortars for grinding foods, including palm fruit, were often discovered within 30 feet of palm groves. This was the case in Andreas, Murray, and Palm Canyons, all located near Palm Springs, California. Charcoal-darkened soil, blackened rock shelter walls, and rock flakes indicative of campsites were found in Tajo Canyon, Baja California Norte, and

in Boundary Canyon, located just north of the U.S. - Mexico border. Rock art was associated with these and many other sites as well. Particularly fine examples of rock art were noted at the West Fork of Palm Canyon, at Corn Spring, and at Andreas Canyon, all in Riverside County, California. Human presence was also indicated by trails that led from valley floors directly to oases. These were easily observable, especially those that led to Travertine Palms in Anza-Borrego Desert State Park and Blue Palm Canyon in Baja California Norte. At Mountain Palm Springs in San Diego County, manmade stone circles, sometimes ten feet in diameter, lay near the mouths of canyons harboring palms.

It became obvious that Indians living within the Sonoran Desert were well aware of the existence of most palm oases. Research conducted by Lowell John Bean in 1984 indicated that a permanent village occupied the mouth of Andreas Canyon, and I suspect that this was the case at most of the large palm oases lying along the eastern base of the Peninsular Ranges of southern and Baja California. Even smaller, more remote palm oases harbored permanent Indian populations, as indicated by archaeological work near the Oasis of Mara at Twentynine Palms, California. That Indians visited and stayed at desert fan palm oases was not surprising. Most oases had permanent surface water; nearly all had water that could be reached by digging. The desert fan palms provided abundant shade, and their transpiring leaves, along with evaporation from moist soil, ponds, or streams, ameliorated the high daytime temperatures in summer.

The Palm as a Resource

In addition to the favorable climate at an oasis, the palms provided an abundance of food and material resources. Although most desert springs or streams

Opposite: Indian petroglyphs at Corn Spring, Riverside County, California.

support cottonwoods, willows, and sycamores, it was probably the desert fan palm that held the greatest attraction of any oasis tree. Although cottonwood branches were occasionally used for building posts, and willow stems were used for bows and large storage baskets, palms provided construction material for dwellings, bows, baskets and clothes as well as wood for tools, ceremonial objects, and fire-starting material.

The dried fruit stems of desert fan palms were useful in starting fires. J. Smeaton Chase in his California Desert Trails, published in 1919, described the process in detail:

Two pieces of dry palm-fruit stem were the tools, one an inch or so broad, length immaterial, the other less than half as thick, about a foot long, and perfectly straight. A few dead leaves were placed in a little heap: the larger stick was laid beside them and held in place by one of the men, a hollow having first been made in the surface of the wood, with a little groove leading from it to the leaves. Then the smaller stick, trimmed to a blunt point, was put to the hollow, and rapidly revolved by rolling between the open hands of the other

Indian. His hands moved down as he rolled, returning again and again to the top. The friction sent a fine stream of wood powder down the groove upon the leaves. In less than two minutes smoke showed at the point of friction, then sparks began to fall on the tinder, and finally a flame was started by blowing. Less than three minutes sufficed for the operation. It was hard work while it lasted, for the fire was endangered by the perspiration caused in kindling it.

The fan-shaped leaves of the desert fan palm are remarkably long-lasting. Hundred-year-old trees often have "skirts" composed of dead leaves that extend from the crown to the ground, completely obscuring the trunk. With this durability in mind, it should not be surprising that native peoples pulled these leaves from the trunks and used them to thatch the roofs and walls of their dwellings. This practice continues today in Baja California, where such thatched roofs remain leakproof at least five years.

Palm fibers were occasionally used to make baskets, although they did not wear as well as those made from the stems of *Juncus* or sumac. Sandals were commonly

Cahuilla Indians demonstrate the art of starting a fire with a palm-fruit stem. Photograph courtesy of Palm Springs Desert Museum.

manufactured from palm leaves and were still worn as footwear when writer/ photographer George Wharton James visited the Cahuilla of the Colorado Desert in the late 1800s. Palm leaf stems were carved into shovels, spoons, and stirring implements.

Parts of the fan palm were also eaten as food. A newspaper article written by C. C. Parry in 1881 mentions that Indians would sometimes cut out and consume the growing tip of palms. Edward Curtis stated that the pith of the crown was a famine food and was boiled before being eaten. Since either practice would probably kill a tree, it would have been devastating to palm groves and was probably not a common occurrence. Young leaf bases were also eaten at times.

By far the most important food resource provided by the palm was its fruit. In late summer and early fall, healthy trees could produce ten fruit stalks per tree with 40 pounds of fruit per stalk. In wet years, the total harvest might average 350,000 fruits, or 350 pounds of fruit per tree. The stalks hung down 6 to 12 feet from the crown, usually out of human reach. Harvesting was accomplished with a long willow pole, notched at one end. A quick twist broke the stalk and brought the fruit clusters to the ground.

Palm fruit was often eaten fresh, and the small, hard seeds spit out. However, Cahuilla women usually sun-dried the fruit and stored it in large ceramic jars. Later, the entire fruit would be ground into flour in bedrock mortars. I found the seeds much too hard to be ground without soaking first, which may explain why Lowell John Bean and Katherine Siva Saubel, in their book *Temalpakh*, relate that the final product consumed was a mush. They also learned that a tea was made by soaking the fruit in water, a possible byproduct of soaking the fruit in preparation for grinding. Victoria Wierick, a Cahuilla, states that jelly was also made from the fruits.

Many other useful plants surrounded

the palm groves, including the most important plant for desert Indians, the honeypod mesquite (*Prosopis glandulosa*). Even today, nearly every oasis harbors this shrub. It cannot compete for space with the faster growing palms, but its longer roots allow it to tap the deep-lying moisture around the oasis margins. Also common at many palm oases were *Juncus*, used in basketmaking, cattail (*Typha* spp.) for food and medicine, and arrowweed (*Pluchea sericea*) used to construct arrow shafts and dwellings.

The Palm in Myth

The palm oasis was obviously a productive environment that offered many attractions to desert peoples. It is not surprising that its dominant and most stately member, the desert fan palm, should play an important role in the myths of the people very familiar with it, the Cahilla of southern California. In his book *Stories and Legends of the Palm Springs Indians* Cahuilla Chief Francisco

A Cahuilla Indian basket, woven of palm fibers. Photograph by Tom Brewster.

Patencio tells how the first palm tree was formed:

One of the head men of the people of Sungrey [legendary ancestors of the Cahuilla] felt that his time was about gone. His years among his people were many, and he must be prepared to go. This man wanted to be a benefit to his people, so he said: 'I am going to be a palm tree. There are no palms in the world. My name shall always be Moul' [palm tree]. So he stood up very straight and very strong and very powerful, and soon the bark of the tree began to grow around him, and the green leaves grew from the top of his head.

Certainly the most profound impact Indians had upon the ecology of palm oases was their practice of deliberately setting palm groves on fire. The relationship between fire and palms is a recurring theme in Cahuilla oral history. In the following account by Chief Patencio, Mukat, the Cahuilla creator, says:

Then when my creation coyote goes for the Rockfire and the Sunfire, you must start to

my creation that is a girl, a very fine girl, Min my wit *the palm, and make a fire out of her.*

Palm Fires

It is not known how the Cahuilla started fires, but it would seem that the practice was carefully supervised and directed by an experienced "fire starter". Dead palm leaves, which may still be affixed to the trunk, are exceedingly flammable. Even moderate winds make for an uncontrollable situation which threatens not only the slow-growing mesquite, but many other valuable food plants as well. An out-of-control fire would have threatened village sites which, as previously described, contained structures covered with dry palm leaves. In a purposive burn situation, it seems reasonable to assume that an attempt would have been made to select a place and time that would maximize a fire's beneficial effects and minimize its harmful ones. For these reasons, I suspect that fires were started only after the onset of winter rains. At this time the fruit would have been harvested and moist

The Cahuilla round house was often constructed and roofed of palm fronds.

conditions would minimize the chances of the fire burning out of control.

Why did the Indians burn these magnificent trees? Three explanations suggested in the literature reveal the adaptive significance of oasis burning. C. C. Parry implies that Indians set fire to palms to facilitate the harvest of fruit by removing the dead skirts. This permitted gatherers to climb the trunk and secure the hanging fruit clusters during fruiting seasons. (While it was probably the only way fruit stalks could be harvested from palms over 40 feet in height, no other author has corroborated this method of harvesting.) A similar purpose for palm burning has been offered by Katherine Saubel, a Cahuilla living on the Morongo Reservation near Banning, California. She states that one of the reasons palm oases were burned was to clean out debris so that the trees could be reached and the fruits easily recovered.

In my studies, I found that walking through a palm oasis which had not experienced flooding or fire in the previous ten years was no easy task. A great deal of material piled up on the oasis floor, including old fruit stalks, fallen trunks, palm fronds, and shrubs. It was difficult, if not occasionally dangerous, to walk on top of this unstable mass. At the very least, someone was likely to slip on a fallen leaf stem and fall head first on the oasis floor, or be smacked in the face after stepping on the curved end of a seven-foot fruit stalk. Collecting the fallen seed from this jumble would also be an arduous task. After ten years of debris buildup, harvesting fruit in palm oases of over twenty trees would become impossible. In short, burning provided access to the palms and their fruit.

A second major reason for palm burning is described by Chief Patencio:

The bugs that hatched in the top of the palm trees, they made the tree sick, and no fruit came. After the trees were set afire and burned, the bugs were killed and the trees gave good fruit.

Katherine Saubel confirmed this explanation, stating that one reason for palm

Above, left: Rock mortars were used to grind dried palm fruit.

Above, right: Palm fruit. The seeds are so hard that even rodents cannot damage them.

burning was to "get rid of the bugs."

The third, perhaps most functional, explanation for palm burning is the increase in the yield of fruit. George Wharton James suggested this in 1906 when he wrote the following account:

The [Cahuilla] Indians used to have most interesting ceremonies in connection with these palms. They tell me that it was their ancient custom each year to set fire to the dead leaves. This rendered the fruit of the palm larger and sweeter.

Patencio states:

It was the medicine men who burned the palm trees so that they could get good fruit.

I have not yet tested whether fire makes palm fruit larger and sweeter. However, in a survey involving 350 palms, those which had burned within the past four years produced 63 percent more fruit than did unburned palms.

Although not previously mentioned in the ethnographic literature, a fourth reason for palm oasis burning is that fire favors palms at the expense of cottonwoods, willows, sycamores, and other oasis plants. A 1926 photograph of Palm Canyon, near Palm Springs, California, shows approximately 82 trees in the area adjacent to Hermit's Bench. In 1984 a photograph taken from the identical angle shows 132 palms. This 62 percent increase is partially attributable to the elimination of cottonwoods from a large portion of the oasis — the result of the Palm Canyon fire of 1946. Fire temporarily removes all other plant species, leaving only the fire-resistant palms. With competition removed, palm seedlings are far more likely to become established. The benefit to the Indians was that a valuable plant species replaced those of less value.

Photographs of palm oases taken prior to 1936 generally reveal trees that had not been burned in fifty or more years. These

same photographs, along with a few early counts of oasis palms by Randall Henderson, indicate that palms were probably declining in numbers prior to World War II. After 1945, the large number of settlers coming into southeastern California and the related increase in human-started fires resulted in the return of a fire regime in palm oases. It is likely that the apparent decline in the number of palms up to World War II was a result of the disappearance of Indians (from disease-caused mortality and forced migrations) from the oasis environment in the late 1800s.

Dispersal of Seeds

Not only did Indians promote the growth of palms by regularly burning the oases, but there is evidence that they were responsible for disseminating the seeds over broad areas of the Sonoran Desert. Chase indicated that many palm oases were actually planted by Indians. The late Harry James told of one group of palms in

Flakes of stone chipped from this stone core were used by Indians as tools for scraping, chopping and cutting.

the San Jacinto Mountains that was initiated by Indians. Cahuilla oral literature also suggests that palms were distributed by their ancestors:

The people carried the seeds to their homes, and palm trees grew from this seed in many places. The palm trees in every place from this first palm tree . . . all, every one of them . . .

A number of palm oases occur so far from the Salton Trough and the eastern base of southern California's Peninsular Range – the center of the desert fan palm's distribution – that animal disperal seems highly improbable. Considering Cahuilla oral history, human dissemination seems the most likely explanation for the existence of oases located in the Kofa Mountains and at Castle Hot Springs in Arizona, Mopah Springs and Twentynine Palms along the southern edge of the Mojave Desert, and Corn Spring in the Sonoran Desert of southeastern California. Furthermore, each of these palm oases lie adjacent to known archaeological sites. It is well known that American Indians transported other useful plant seeds over long distances; the spread of maize throughout the New World is only one example. The easily transported seeds of the desert fan palm lent themselves very well to human introduction, as they readily germinate under a variety of temperatures and soil regimens.

It appears that the desert fan palm is an excellent example of a plant species whose ecology can best be understood in light of its interaction with Indian people. Indeed, in many instances it appears that Indians have taken this species to the geographical limits of its range. Randall Henderson speculates that Indians also planted palms at one of the highest altitude oases, Dos Palmas Spring in the Santa Rosa Mountains of southern California. In addition, Indian-initiated fires undoubtedly maintained palms in far greater numbers than would have occurred under natural conditions. It is not inconceivable that the

entire status of palms in the Sonoran Desert of southeastern California might have been vastly different were it not for the Indians' use and management of this spectacular desert plant.

Bedrock mortars, such as these in Andreas Canyon near Palm Springs, were used to grind palm fruit.

CHAPTER FOUR:

The Giant Palm Boring Beetle

One of California's most unusual insects is the giant palm boring beetle, *Dinapate wrightii*. At two inches in length, it is truly a giant, nearly twice as large as any other bostrichid beetle, with a huge head and powerful jaws that could easily draw blood were they to clamp onto human skin. The fact that the beetles feed in the trunks of fan palms hidden away in the remote oases of the Sonoran Desert of southeastern California explains the lack of knowledge concerning this beetle's ecology, and raises interesting questions about its dispersal and distribution.

Dinapate was unknown to science until 1886 when the beetle and larva were described by G. H. Horn from specimens found by naturalist William G. Wright. Wright claimed he had obtained his beetles in the Mojave Desert but refused to divulge the precise collecting locality. The late Edmund Jaeger indicated that Wright was purposely vague about the destinations of his desert collecting trips, and though entomologist friends occasionally tried to follow, he would always elude them. According to Jaeger, Wright's secrecy was designed to assure a high

selling price for his beetles, which brought up to $1,000 a pair from European museums. For 13 years Wright kept his secret and the habitat of *Dinapate* remained a mystery.

It was not until 1899 that a paper was published which revealed the habits and life history of the giant palm boring beetle. Two years before, Henry Hubbard of Los Angeles had found a specimen of *Dinapate* beneath a desert fan palm, *Washingtonia filifera*, near Palm Springs, California. Upon further investigation he discovered that the huge, pale-yellow larvae lived in the native palms and ate extensive tunnels through the trunks. With the publication of this information in *Entomological News*, the mystery was solved. Within a few years, hundreds of specimens made their way into museums throughout the country. (In 1986 a new species of *Dinapate* was described by Kenneth Cooper of the University of California at Riverside. Named *Dinapate hughleechi*, in honor of Hugh Leech of the California Academy of Sciences, it is known from the Mexican states of Tamaulipas and San Luis Potosi and infests the trunks of the palm, *Sabal texana*.)

Dinapate is impressive not only because of its size but also because of what appears to be its enormous disproportionate head. However, upon close examination this segment is found to be comprised of a normal-sized head which fits into a huge bulbous thorax. The unusual thorax seems to function as a wedge which is jammed against the ceiling of the tunnel allowing the jaws to be pushed deeply into the wood. The thorax is well formed in the larva but cannot be seen as it is covered by the grub's skin-like cuticle.

A second striking feature of *Dinapate* is its set of two posterior horns. Although present in both sexes, the males' horns are considerably longer. The function of the horns is not known but they could possibly aid in sex recognition when

Opposite: Horseshoe Palms, on the San Andreas Fault in the Coachella Valley Preserve. The tallest, oldest palms are least resistant to damage from Dinapate wrightii, *the giant palm boring beetle.*

31

several male beetles are in tight quarters fighting over a female. Interestingly, these structures force the recently metamorphosed adult palm borer to exit its tree backwards. Since the horns make the posterior width greater than the head or thorax, the only assurance that it has constructed a large enough exit hole is to get the back end out first. A head-first exit runs the risk of having the legs flailing helplessly in midair because the horns and abdomen are stuck in the tunnel.

It is not clear just how many years *Dinapate* larvae spend in their palm nests. The late Nelson Baker, a curator at the Palm Springs Desert Museum, suggested that the time period from egg to adult beetle lasted from three to five years. However, a carved human figure made from a palm log was seven years old when an adult *Dinapate* emerged from its dime-sized exit hole — thus under certain conditions the larvae may persist for seven years within hewn logs.

The precise factors which control the beetle's rate of development are un-

known but certainly temperature and condition of the trees are important. Beetles do vary in size and no doubt this variation is affected by the quality of the environment in which they mature. Smaller-than-normal individuals, for example, may emerge from damaged palms or perhaps ones that are overcrowded with larvae.

When the larva is ready to pupate — in April or May — it constructs a larval chamber about one inch from the exterior surface of the trunk. This chamber is really just a wider-than-normal tunnel that provides sufficient space for the beetle to turn around after it chews an exit hole. About seven weeks elapse between pupation and emergence, but a portion of this time may incorporate a resting period for the adult. Eventually, the adult chews its way out of the trunk and through the leaf skirt, if the fronds have not been burned away. *Dinapate* only emerges after dark. Work by Kenneth Cooper suggests that the beetles recognize night by a drop in ambient temperature. The advantages of a nocturnal emergence are twofold: To

An adult palm boring beetle, Dinapate wrightii, *shown about twice life size.*

avoid predators and to escape hot daytime temperatures.

Both Cooper and Baker found that males and females show no interest in each other upon emergence. Not until a few days later, when the female begins to tunnel into the crown of a palm, do the sexes become receptive. The female enters the crown by chewing into a leaf base and constructs her nest chamber at the end of a tunnel several inches in length. It is at this time that a male shows interest in a female, and in fact, several males may pursue a single female into the nest chamber. Presumably, mating takes place there. A female lays from 400 to 500 white eggs, each measuring about two millimeters long by one millimeter wide.

At one time it was thought the desert fan palm was the only palm species in which *Dinapate wrightii* could be found. Certainly it seems to be the beetles' overwhelming choice between ornamental and naturally-occurring palms in the Sonoran Desert of southeastern California. In fact, in the 151 *Washingtonia filifera* groves that I have examined, all but 12 possessed trees that showed signs of *Dinapate*. I have personally examined several other palm species including *W. robusta* from Baja California and *Brahea nitada* from Sonora, Mexico, and have yet to find *D. wrightii* in these. However, on three occasions specimens of *Brahea armata*, the blue fan palm from Baja California, have been discovered with *Dinapate* exit holes, indicating that the beetles do successfully utilize palms other than *W. filifera*. (There is also one report of their attacking commerical date palms as well.)

Of special interest to me was the impact of *Dinapate* on the health and longevity of desert fan palms. There are four obvious causes of palm mortality: extended drought, flood, fire and beetle damage. Drying out of the soil is probably the most significant cause of death for seedlings, and numerous mature palms in Wentworth Canyon near Palm Springs died as a result of a 30-year drought which ended in 1976. A single flash flood can uproot hundreds of palms in such places as Cloudburst Canyon, which drains the Sierra Juarez of Baja California

Far left: Larva of the palm boring beetle.

Left: The beetle's head is just visible as it begins to widen its exit hole.

Norte. Each palm oasis experiences fire, but the mortality of adult palms is low: less than one percent were lost in the fire which occurred in the canyons surrounding Palm Springs in 1980.

About 45 percent of palms over 35 feet in height (and less than one percent of fruit-bearing trees under 20 feet) harbor *Dinapate* exit holes. There is no question that the beetles damage these palms by chewing through the vascular tissue and interrupting the flow of water and nutrients up and down the trunks. There is also no question that their exit holes make the palms more vulnerable to fire by increasing the exposed area of the trunk and thus further the extent of heat damage. I have also found many adult palms (of a variety of heights) that have expired not from drought, flood or fire but from the ravages of *Dinapate*. In such cases there may be several hundred exit holes and the trunks are hardly more than a column of sawdust.

The exact percentage of palms killed by *Dinapate* cannot be determined, since a fallen palm log with exit holes does not necessarily indicate beetle-caused death. However, by examining hundreds of dead standing trees, I have calculated that in oases not subject to severe floods, 70 percent of the adult palms are killed outright by beetles and many remaining trees are killed by fire made more harmful because of *Dinapate* exit holes. The percentage can vary tremendously depending upon the location of the palm oasis and the frequency of fire.

Of special interest is the fact that although many trees have exit holes, a few seem to have unusually large concentrations, giving the impression that some trees are more attractive to egg-laying females than others. I have observed that such trees are usually the tallest and probably the oldest palms in the groves. The older trees would have had the greatest opportunity of being the recipients of ovipositing females. Most tall living palms do not have numerous

Exit holes made by palm boring beetles in a dead palm at West Indian Palms, Coachella Valley Preserve.

beetles holes and most tall dead palms do, reinforcing the idea that very old trees are more likely to be attacked than young ones. These latter observations suggest the palms have some kind of defense against the beetles but that this defense deteriorates with age. (Since palms are monicots they do not have annual growth rings to help determine age as do conifers and dicots. Thus the age of an individual palm can only be surmised by a knowledge of growth rate, condition of the tree, and a review of historical photographs.)

One of the surprising things about these beetles is their apparent ability to disperse from one isolated palm oasis to another, sometimes flying over distances of several miles. *Dinapate* exit holes have been found in the vast majority of palm oases in southeastern California and northeastern Baja California, and some are more than 20 kilometers apart. The only two explanations for this distribution are that the beetles have (1) been in the vicinity since the groves first came into existence or (2) arrived later after the palms became established. (With the possible exception of palm groves in the

Kofa Mountains of western Arizona, desert fan palms became established at remote springs by the long-distance dispersal of their seeds by coyotes, humans or perhaps birds.) If the beetles arrived after the establishment of a grove, then random chance or scent are the only explanation for their arrival. Sight must be excluded since the beetles are practically blind and disperse at night.

What are the odds that both a male and female would accidentally fly into an uninhabited grove within a few days of each other and initiate a new colony of palm boring beetles? Undoubtedly, this could have happened once or twice, but common sense tells us that the scenario cannot be used to explain the beetle's presence in every palm grove in which it occurs.

Scent attraction is a tempting explanation. The ability of salmon to "smell" their way home through thousands of miles of ocean waters to the stream where they were born is well documented. Certain female moths are also known to produce odors which attract males from miles away. Perhaps desert fan palms have an odor that can be detected by the beetles.

Recently the presence or absence of *Dinapate* has assisted in determining the age of certain desert fan palm oases— specifically those groves far removed from the center of the palm's distribution along the San Andreas fault and in the canyons draining the desert slopes of the Peninsular Ranges. Some naturalists believe these remote oases (such as Mopah Spring, Warm Springs and Castle Creek) are relict palm groups that have been present since the warmer moister Pliocene Epoch when palms were more widespread and abundant than they are today. If this were so, there should have been ample opportunity for the beetles to fly the short distances necessary to reach every neighboring grove. Conversely, if the groves are not relicts but are of recent origin, then they would probably not be occupied because the groves have always been separated by too many kilometers of hostile desert terrain to be reached by *Dinapate*. Mopah Spring is the least remote of the three oases mentioned and has no beetles. It lies 56 miles northeast of Corn Spring, the nearest palm oasis

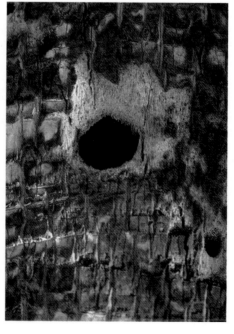

Left: The common flicker is known to nest in dead, standing palm trunks.

Right: The large hole, center, in this palm was enlarged — after the palm burned — by a woodpecker. The smaller hole, lower right, is a beetle exit hole.

Canyon of the
Hidden Spring,
Anza-Borrego
Desert State Park.
Note the dead,
standing palm
(right of center)
that has been killed
by palm boring
beetles.

harboring *Dinapate*. With but one exception—palms in the Kofa Mountains—very remote groves do not harbor beetle populations, thus suggesting that such groves are of recent origin.

Palm grove fires started by lightning or vandals are responsible for much *Dinapate* mortality. Even though the palms usually survive the blaze, larvae which have tunneled to the outer edge are killed by the intense heat. In those instances where the palm is killed but the trunk is not consumed by flames, beetles in the center of the tree often survive. In such situations it seems the larvae must change into adults within one year, as living grubs are never found in fire-killed trunks that are more than one year old. The necessity of their rapid exit is probably a result of the palm interior drying out and the blackened surface, both of which result in higher-than-normal temperatures in the trunk. Indeed, the beetles seem unusually active in these situations, and on several occasions I have been able to hear the rapidly chewing larvae while standing several feet from the charred trunk! Presumably, the warm temperatures allow the larvae to increase their metabolic rates and race through their life cycle before the tree dries out entirely. The uncharred walls of exit holes that commonly appear in old burned palms indicate that beetles do survive in fire-killed palms. Interestingly, the Cahuilla Indians regularly set fire to palm groves, in part to rid the trees of their beetles. Such a management strategy would be effective and important to a people who relied upon the palms for food, shelter and household materials.

The only predators of *Dinapate* are birds, specifically the Common Flicker, Ladder-backed and Gila Woodpeckers. All three locate larvae tunneling close to the exterior by listening to them chew. Evidence of a capture site often shows up as a doughnut-like pattern with a circle of small holes and a large hole in the center where the grub was located and with-drawn. The pecking of such small test holes may cause a larva to reveal its precise location when it attempts to escape by chewing deep into the interior.

Not only does *Dinapate* provide food for woodpeckers, it also facilitates the construction of their nests. Living desert fan palm trunks are too resistant for woodpeckers to peck out cavities. Hence their nests are almost always restricted to dead standing palms — and only those which show numerous *Dinapate* exit holes. It is these trees which are soft enough to attract breeding woodpeckers intent on constructing a new nest cavity. Of course in later years these cavities may also be used by other avian species such as House Finches, American Kestrels, European Starlings and owls.

Another animal that benefits from *Dinapate's* exit holes is the Southern California carpenter bee, *Xylocopa californica*. The females of this insect lay their eggs inside the empty exit tunnels and may be seen almost every spring day entering the beetle holes to provide food for their developing young. In some areas these may be the only suitable nesting sites for the bees.

The giant palm boring beetle is an excellent example of the often complex and subtle relationships between an organism and its environment. As just described, the presence of many other animals in the palm oasis is facilitated by, perhaps dependent on, *Dinapate*. The vitality of the groves themselves is based upon a continuous replacement of older palms by younger palms—a cycle that is enhanced if not perpetuated by the activities of this seldom-observed but fascinating insect.

Clockwise from top: The Western Yellow Bat roosts only in palms; the Common Kingsnake is the snake most often found in desert fan palm oases; a California Treefrog; the Paper Wasp often builds its nest on the underside of a palm leaf.

Top left:
A Greater
Roadrunner has
caught a side-
blotched lizard in
the palm oasis.

Above: Male
Hooded Oriole.

Left: Young
Hooded Orioles in
their nest,
constructed of palm
frond fragments.

CHAPTER FIVE:

Palms of Fire

One reason for the success of the desert fan palm in its hostile environment is its ability to withstand fire. Of course, most of us would not associate the desert with wildfires — after all, what is there to burn? Such environments, by definition, are sparsely vegetated. In fact desert plants are generally so widely spaced that the ignition of one plant does not necessarily mean those around it catch fire. Like roads that often halt the spread of fire, the desert is one huge fire break without continuous stands of fuel that might otherwise carry a fire uninterrupted across a large area.

How, then, does a palm oasis catch fire? Once in a great while, perhaps every few decades, lightning can be expected to strike a tall oasis palm. The palm, partly because of its height and partly because trees in general carry a strong negative electrical charge, can be struck by lightning and burst into flame. The fronds are highly flammable and ignite more readily than even tissue paper. Chris Moser of the Riverside Municipal Museum observed a lightning bolt strike a *Washingtonia* palm. He related that the top of the palm literally exploded upon impact, sending flaming leaves in all directions. Such an event would certainly ensure that an entire oasis became engulfed in flames.

Richard Vogl, a botanist at California State University, Los Angeles, has asserted that a palm oasis fire might start in a pile of decaying plant matter on the oasis floor; the heat of decay plus hot summer temperatures resulting in ignition. The late author Earle Stanley Gardner suggested that hanging leaf stalks rubbed together during high winds could also start a palm oasis fire by sending sparks into the dry palm skirts, causing them to burst into flame. However, there has never been a single eyewitness account of either of the latter two factors starting a palm oasis fire.

Today, most oasis fires are started by humans either accidentally or as an act of vandalism; there are many accurate accounts of vandalism-started fires. The Dry Falls fires of 1980 which burned four palm oases near Palm Springs, California, was started by two young boys playing with matches. The palm oasis at Corn Springs in Riverside County's Chuckwalla Mountain burned in 1979 when campers built a campfire under the dry skirt of one of the trees. The palms at Hidden Spring in the Mecca Hills were torched in 1977 by several young men—just for fun.

Although many palm oases are located far out on the desert surrounded by sparsely vegetated terrain, most large palm oases (and in fact most wild desert fan palms) grow in canyons at the eastern base of the Peninsular Ranges. These ranges, including the San Jacinto, Santa Rosa and Cuyamaca Mountains, receive relatively abundant winter moisture on their western or windward slopes but become quite arid on their eastern or "leeward" slopes. The canyons on the eastern flanks often have year-round streams as a result of the huge watershed and high, snow-covered peaks. The palms and other oasis-associated plant species such as cottonwoods, willows and sycamores are abundant at the lower reaches of the canyons, but give way to alders and eventually pines and new species of willows at the upper eleva-

Palm Canyon, near Palm Springs, California, is the largest palm oasis in North America.

tions. Thus there is a continuous fuel corridor up and down the canyon. A fire which starts anywhere in the high country, or many miles away on the western slopes, may eventually reach the lower canyon bottoms along the eastern sides of the mountains. I term these contact fires since the burn does not originate in the palm oasis but rather spreads there as a result of the oasis coming in contact with other plant communities also subject to fire.

Desert plants often show little capacity to survive fire. This isn't surprising—fire is so rare in desert environments that plant species have not had much, if any, selective pressure to adapt to a fire regime. This is quite unlike chaparral plants on the western slopes of the Peninsular Ranges in southern California. Many of these species have evolved strategies for perpetuating their species after a fire. The manzanita, for example, sprouts new branches from its root crown. *Ceanothus* (wild lilac) has seeds which germinate best when they have been scorched by fire. These adaptations, or at least their refinement, have evolved

over a long period of time in an environment where fires are relatively frequent.

Why then is the desert fan palm so adept at surviving fires? Probably in part because its occurrence in today's desert is relatively recent. It, or at least its immediate ancestors, survived in habitats where fire played a greater role than in many of the isolated oases where it exists today. Equally important in understanding its tolerance of fire is the kinds of adaptations shown by its close relatives. As a member of the Palm Family, *Arecaceae*, it is pre-adapted to a fire regime. Many, if not most, palm species are tolerant of fire. As monocots, they have their sensitive vascular tissue strewn throughout the trunk, not confined to a narrow cambium layer just beneath the bark as is the case with conifers and dicot trees. Many fires may be sufficiently hot to destroy the vascular tissue just beneath the bark, but rarely is a fire hot enough to kill the vascular tissue in the center of a palm. There are many palm species which do quite well in environments where fires are common, such as Australia's savanna or Africa's Serengeti Plains. The desert fan palm is simply one

Willis Palms, located in the Coachella Valley Preserve, during the 1983 fire. Photograph by Richard Misrach.

42

of many examples of a palm species that is tolerant of fire.

In fact the only specific adaptation shown by this species, and not found in all palms, is its very smooth bark. Smooth bark has the advantage of exposing a minimum of surface area to a fire's heat, thus minimizing damage. Some members of the palm family, such as date palms in the genus *Phoenix*, have rough bark and therefore have trunks that are more susceptible to fire damage.

Whether as a result of accident, vandalism, or lightning most palm oases catch fire sooner or later. I have visited all 151 of the known desert fan palm oases and only nine appear to have never burned. At least part of the cause is a result of the characteristics of the desert fan palm itself. Palms burn, and burn readily. The ever-present water and warm temperatures through much of the year promote a long growing season and a large production of fuel. The resultant ground litter, combined with the ever-present threat of ignition through vandalism or lightning—make it not surprising that 85% of all wild palm oases have burned within the last fifty years.

Within the last hundred years, 94% have burned.

On the afternoon of February 20, 1983, vandals started a fire in an oasis known as Willis Palms located along the San Andreas Fault, near Palm Springs, California. The fire lasted for over an hour and was intense. Seventeen years had passed since the last conflagration. The dry fronds, spent fruit stalks and fallen trunks provided a large amount of fuel on which the flames could feed. Within one hour all 604 mature palms had burned, leaving only a six-inch carpet of gray ash on the oasis floor and hundreds of fire-blackened trunks. The devastation seemed complete. To the uninitiated, the palm oasis appeared to have been destroyed.

Five months after the holocaust, I returned to Willis Palms. To my amazement, nearly every palm had sprouted an entire new crown of green fronds. In fact, I was able to document the death of only three mature palms as a result of the intense heat of the fire — a mortality rate of less than 1%! Many of the palms were producing massive amounts of fruit and clearly would be the only plant species to

Willis Palms one year after the fire. Nearly every palm has survived.

This resilient young palm survived an oasis fire, and shows new growth from the crown.

set seed that year. The palm grove had not been destroyed at all, but had rejuvenated itself in grand fashion. So far as I know, no palm oasis has ever been permanently destroyed by fire. Every palm grove or cluster has survived even the most intensive blaze.

It is true that small *filiferas* may succumb to fire. The thickness of a young palm trunk is not great and the fire's heat can penetrate to the center, thus destroying all conducting tissue. However, desert fan palms grow quickly. Within ten years following germination, a palm can be expected to be ten feet tall and possess a trunk diameter exceeding eighteen inches; usually sufficient to withstand a "normal" burn. Only if intense fires occurred once every ten years for at least six decades would the ability of the palms to replace themselves be threatened. It is doubtful, however, that intense fires could occur with such frequency and regularity.

It is known that the Cahuilla Indians of the southern California deserts set fire to palm oases to clean the oasis floor of debris and permit the harvesting of the trees' fruit. Co-researchers and I also learned that ten years after a fire, the fallen flower stalks, fronds, and trunks pile up again and make it difficult to walk through an oasis. Twenty years after a fire the debris is so deep and unstable that walking through an oasis can actually be hazardous. One may step on the end of a two-meter flower stalk, resulting in a blow to the head akin to stepping onto a hoe. (Among our research team members it took an embarrassing number of mishaps to learn this bit of palm lore.) In addition, rattlesnakes use the litter as shelter. We met up with these oasis inhabitants many times. It was easy for us to understand why Indians burned oases, perhaps every ten years, certainly every twenty.

Not only does *Washingtonia filifera* survive fire, it seems to thrive under a fire regime. Hidden Palms, near the floor of the central Coachella Valley, burned three times between 1939 and 1979, the greatest fire frequency of any palm oasis I know. One might expect that young palms might be eliminated—yet Hidden Palms had the highest ratio of young to mature palms of any palm oasis. The first fire, in 1939 did away with all of the fuel which had covered the oasis floor and prevented the germination and survival of young palms. After the fire the adult palms produced seed which ultimately fell onto the barren oasis floor, now moister than it had ever been before the fire. This was a result of the elimination of water-using plants for several months after the fire and then only a partial return to "normalcy" as the mature palms developed new crowns and began using groundwater again. The moist soil was now fully exposed to the sun after the fire eliminated the shade-producing plants. Rich with mineral-laden ash, the soil provided superb germinating conditions for the palm seeds which sprouted like grass over the oasis floor.

The story of the Hidden Palms fire of 1972 would not be complete without mentioning that the Riverside County Fire Department did respond to the fire. By the time they arrived there was little to do; the oasis had burned up. However, to ensure that no flareups would occur they cut down twenty of the still-smoldering palms. They reasoned that the palms had been killed by the fire and by chopping them down they could apply water more easily to the burning crowns! Fortunately, the department has been informed that palms are not killed by fire and the practice of chopping down smoldering palms has been discontinued.

Desert fan palms can add up to two feet of trunk per year, so by the time the next fire struck Hidden Palms in 1972 many of the young palms had thick enough trunks to withstand a modest fire. And the fire of 1979 was modest. With little debris accumulation in just seven years, the fire was not hot. It lasted a brief 50 minutes

and killed only a handful of young palms.

Once again the stage was set for a second crop of young palms. Seeds were produced the following fall and again fell on moist, cleared soil. By 1983 there were 264 young palms compared with 191 adult palms; a ratio of seven to five.

I cannot say at what frequency fire no longer promotes an increase in the number of palms in an oasis — only that

Burned palms produce a healthy crop of fruit the season after an oasis fire.

no oasis seems to have yet reached a fire frequency that has anything but long-term beneficial effects, insofar as the palms are concerned.

What fire does effect is the plant species composition of the oasis. It favors palms over cottonwoods, willows, sycamores and most other perennials since these latter trees (or at least their above-ground portions) are destroyed by fire. An absence of fire allows other plant species to gain a foothold and compete for dominance in an oasis with the palms. Thus the Fremont cottonwood (*Populus fremontii*) and species of willow (*Salix*) are large and relatively abundant in oases that have not burned for several decades and are scarce or even absent in oases that burn more frequently.

Curious about the significance of fire in palm oasis ecology, my colleagues and I set about comparing the fruit production of burned palms with unburned palms. We found that mature palms which had been burned recently were likely to grow 11 fruit stalks (spadices) compared with 7 fruit stalks for unburned palms. Now we are aware that the amount of seeds attached to any given fruit stalk can vary from about 1,000 to over 30,000, but our observations indicated that if anything, the fruit stalks produced by burned palms were more heavily laden with fruit. Therefore not only does fire promote the growth of young palms, but it also results in a significantly greater seed production on the part of mature palms.

Why this might be so is a somewhat more difficult question to answer. Clues are provided by desert fan palms growing under cultivated conditions. This palm species is widely planted as an ornamental. In fact, it is likely that the desert fan palm is one of the most widely planted palm species in the world—I have seen it along boulevards in Sydney, Australia and Nairobi, Kenya as well as southern European cities. These ornamentals were found to produce even more fruit stalks than burned palms growing wild in California desert oases. This fact suggested that it might not be burning per se that caused a burned palm to produce more spadices, but that some facet of the environment that was duplicated in an ornamental situation was the cause. Ornamental palms are typically given a regular and reliable supply of water and are more or less free of competition from other plant species. This situation occurs to wild palms after a fire. The fire results in more water reaching nearer the surface due to elimination of competing plant species, and may enable the palms to grow more fruit stalks.

Fire may also help the dissemination of the seeds. It was Randall Henderson, an early naturalist and desert explorer, who first pointed out the importance of coyotes in the dissemination of palm seeds. Coyotes eat the fruits for their tasty skin and flesh, but cannot digest the rock-hard seeds and ultimately pass them intact in their droppings. Experiments at the Palm Springs Desert Museum have shown that the seeds are twice as likely to germinate after having traveled through a coyote. Fruits are hard to find when dropped into the rubble on an unburned oasis, but

These seedling palms were generated by palm fruit seeds in a coyote dropping.

readily available if fire has cleared the floor of debris. Thus fire may facilitate the finding of palm fruits by any fruit-eater, not just the coyote.

Fire may also help the palms in another way. Other than floodwaters raging through canyons where desert fan palms occur, it is the attack of the Giant Palm Boring Beetle, *Dinapate wrightii*, that causes the most palm mortality as a result of its devouring the woody interior of the palm. A fire can kill beetle larvae tunneling close to the exterior and can also prohibit the successful infestation of the crown of the palm by the female beetle should the fire occur in June when *Dinapate* reproduces. The reduction of beetle numbers in an infested palm is likely to mean a longer life and more time in which a palm can produce seed.

In summary, it is worth noting just what happens after an oasis fire. Typically, all above-ground plant life is destroyed except for the adult palm trees. Any cotton-woods, sycamores, willows, mesquite, or

tamarisk trees or shrubs are destroyed down to ground level. Most of these other, potential competitors have the capacity to survive but do so by producing new shoots from their crowns or roots. With the exception of the shrub tamarisk, *Tamarix ramosissima*, (a recently introduced species) it will be several years before any competitor plants will be able to produce seeds. Thus the desert fan palm is the only native plant species to maintain adult plants capable of producing viable seed at the first opportunity after the fire. This gives it an edge over every other plant species in the oasis and is an important factor in its ability to maintain a strong foothold in the oases of the California deserts.

The coyote helps spread the desert fan palm by eating the fruit at one oasis and later depositing digested seeds at another location.

Inset: coyote droppings containing palm seeds.

James W. Cornett is
Curator of Natural Science
at the Palm Springs Desert
Museum in Palm Springs,
California. He holds both
B.A. and M.S. degrees in
biology and is the author of
over 25 papers dealing
with the ecology of desert
fan palm oases. He has
written several books,
including *Wildlife of the
North American Deserts*
and *Death Valley:
A Pictorial History.*